Heartfelt Poems

of

Inspiration

Andrea E. McDowell

To order additional copies of this book, contact:
Xlibris
1-888-795-4274
www.Xlibris.com
Orders@Xlibris.com

Dedication

I dedicate my writing to my late mother (Jeannette Strong Phillips). Inspired by the faith that she exhibited through her battle with cancer and heart disease, I expressed my feelings through poetry and preaching.

Table of Contents

A FATHER

A father is so precious,
Just like our own dear mother;
A father is so precious,
He is like a real close brother;
A father is so precious,
Sometimes it's hard to tell;
A father is so precious,
Although he sometimes yells;
A father is so precious,
He is as strong as can be;
A father is so precious,
Because he is so dear to me;
A father is so precious,
Because God has made that so;
A father is so precious,
We will never, ever let go.

A SONG

A song from Zion is heard from above,
Always sing it with feelings of love;
A song from Heaven is felt in your heart,
Always sing it and do your part;
A song from God has beauty and fame,
Always sing it to praise his name;
A song from Glory ring's loud and clear,
Always sing it because God is so near;
A song from your Savior can only bless,
Always sing it and do your best;
A song from your Master as you can see,
Is Glory Divine and sweet as can be;
A song from Zion is heard from above,
Always sing it with feelings of love.

COMFORT

There is comfort,
When you need a friend;
There is comfort,
In someone you can depend;
There is comfort,
When you are feeling down;
There is comfort,
In someone who is around;
There is comfort,
When you know this wonderful man;
There is comfort,
Because he is on every hand;
There is comfort,
When you know Jesus Christ;
There is comfort,
When he is in your life.

COMMITMENT

Commit your way unto the Lord,
Our Lord and Savior Jesus Christ;
Meditate on his word,
Many scriptures you can believe;
In righteousness you will receive,
Trust in him and keep the faith;
Mainly in God's Holy Grace,
Enduring all things until the end;
Not even knowing where to begin,
Trials and tribulations on ever hand;
Just remember your commitment and stand.

COURAGE

When things get you down,
Just find some courage;
When people talk about you,
Just find some courage;
When your friends forsake you,
Just find some courage;
When life is not fair,
Just find some courage;
When you have lost your way,
Just find some courage;
And when you think you have had enough,
Just find some courage;
You can be real tough,
If you just find some courage.

DO NOT TRY TO HARD

Live life as it comes,
But do not try to hard;
Use the knowledge you have gained,
But do not try to hard;
Take one day at a time,
But do not try to hard;
Remember the mistakes you have made,
But do not try to hard;
Stay on neutral ground,
But do not try to hard;
Give respect to get it in return,
But do not try to hard;
Love your enemies in spite of it all,
But do not try to hard;
Try not to fall to far below,
But do not try to hard;
Keep your hand in God's hand,
And you won't have to try to hard.

ETERNITY FOREVER

Eternity is forever,
Life's other side you see;
Eternity is forever,
Christ was born for you and me;
Eternity is forever,
He lived to set us free;
Eternity is forever,
He suffered for us tremendously;
Eternity is forever,
Because Christ died for you and me;
Eternity is forever.

FAMILY

A family starts with a husband and a wife,
They bond together to stay for life;
One child is born to join the union,
A family is blessed only with God;
Have the faith to stay together,
No matter how hard things may seem;
A family is blessed daily with God,
A family can be just a father and a child;
Just remember you are still one,
A family can be just a mother and a child;
But as long as you live you are still one,
A family can be just a husband and a wife;
Realizing a family has God for their guide,
A family can never, ever be broken;
Unless there is something standing in the way,
Go down on your knees, fast and pray;
A family is sure to stay in God's Holy Way.

FORGIVENESS

Forgiving is hard, I must say,
But Jesus said you must trust and obey;
Forgiving is hard, when you've been hurt,
But Jesus said you must make it work;
Forgiving is hard, it can stand in your way,
But Jesus said just fast and pray;
Forgiving is hard, without real love,
But it was done far, far above;
Forgiving is hard, but it's something we must do,
And Jesus said, he will see us through.

HANG IN THERE

Things are going to get better,
Just hang in there;
Things may seem a little dim right now,
Just hang in there;
Don't know which way to go,
Just hang in there;
You will soon be able to know,
What to do and where to go;
Who to see and what to be,
Just hang in there;
No matter how hard things may seem,
Jesus Christ has been there for you;
Remember what he did that Friday afternoon,
He stayed right there, so you can do it too;
Just hang in there.

HOW I GOT OVER

When I look far above,
At the clouds filled with love;
Then I realize how I got over,
As I search deep down in my heart;
And I have really did my part,
Then I realize how I got over;
When I see the tall rough mountain,
And just beyond it, there is a fountain;
Then I realize how I got over,
I know for sure where I have been;
And I promised myself not to go there again,
Then I realize how I got over;
My God has showed along the way,
That he is here and here to stay;
Just to show me, how I got over.

IT IS NEVER TO LATE

It is never to late,
To say I am sorry;
It is never to late,
To start over again;
It is never to late,
To love the ones you hate;
It is never to late,
To help the ones that despise you;
It is never to late,
To trust the people that misuse you;
It is never to late,
If you want to be friends;
It is never to late,
To except Jesus Christ;
And it is never to late,
For you to start a new life.

LIFE

Life is something we should cherish,
As every precious moment passes;
We should live our life day by day,
So we can handle whatever comes our way;
God gave his life so we may live,
He sent his son so we could see;
Just how hard life would be,
Through the storm and through the rain;
Don't live your life as a game,
Walk with God along the way;
Hold his hand, fast and pray,
Live your life day by day;
And you will stay in God's Holy Way.

NO REGRETS

You get up in the morning,
And you have no regrets;
You prepare yourself for the day,
And you have no regrets;
You keep your chin up along the way,
And you have no regrets;
Somethings may happen during the day,
But you have no regrets;
Whether good or bad,
You keep a smile on your face;
And you have no regrets,
The end of the day comes;
You say your prays,
And you have no regrets.

ON THE OTHER SIDE

ON THE OTHER SIDE,
THERE IS A WONDERFUL PLACE;
ON THE OTHER SIDE,
FILLED WITH PLENTY OF GRACE;
ON THE OTHER SIDE,
THERE IS A MARVELOUS LIFE;
ON THE OTHER SIDE,
WITH HOPE THAT THINGS WILL TURN OUT RIGHT;
ON THE OTHER SIDE,
THE STREETS ARE PAVED WITH GOLD;
ON THE OTHER SIDE,
YOU WILL NEVER GET OLD;
ON THE OTHER SIDE,
THERE ARE NO BILLS TO PAY;
NO ONE TO SAY IT IS TO LATE,
YOU CAN WALK THROUGH ONE OF THE GATES;
ON THE OTHER SIDE,
YOU DON'T HAVE TO WORRY;
ABOUT WHAT TOMORROW WILL BRING,
YOU CAN JUST RELAX;
AND BE YOURSELF,
ON THE OTHER SIDE.

PREJUDICE IS JUST A WORD

PREJUDICE IS JUST A WORD,
WE'VE ALL FOUND IT SOMEWHERE,
IT IS A WORD WE OFTEN MISUSE,
FOR SOME STRANGE REASON;
PREJUDICE IS JUST A WORD,
IT IS THERE FOR COINVENIENCE ONLY,
BUT DO WE REALLY KNOW WHAT TO SAY;
IS IT THE CLOTHES ON OUR BACK,
OR JUST HOW WE'VE BEEN LOOKED AT;
IS IT THE COLOR OF OUR SKIN,
OR JUST WHERE WE HAVE BEEN;
IS IT THE COMPANY THAT WE KEEP,
OR IS IT JUST A LITTLE TO DEEP;
IS IT THE NEIGHBOR WE HAVE NEXT DOOR,
OR DO WE EVEN CARE ANYMORE;
PREJUDICE IS JUST A WORD,
IS IT SOMETHING DOWN WITHIN,
THAT MAKES US FEEL THE NEED TO WIN;
IS IT SOMETHING THAT GIVES US PRIDE,
AN ORDER TO JUST STAY ALIVE;
OR IS IT JUST THE FACT,
THAT WE ARE JUST ALIKE DEEP DOWN INSIDE,
AND COME TO KNOW THAT,
PREJUDICE IS JUST A WORD.

PRIDE

Pride can sometimes stand in your way,
It will be there each and every day;
Pride can sometimes make you do things,
No matter how many heart aches it brings;
Pride can turn your thoughts aside,
But it will make you want to abide;
Pride can make you walk out on faith,
Living for Jesus and in his grace;
Pride will make you want to go on,
It makes you feel like you have been born;
Pride will make you pray everyday,
That you stay in God's Holy Way.

REJOICE

Rejoice and be glad,
Jesus has died to make it so;
Rejoice and praise his name,
Jesus knows our every need;
Rejoice and remember that night,
When Jesus hung to save our souls;
Rejoice and love the father,
Which is in heaven and in earth;
Rejoice and praise his name,
For we know this is not a game;
Rejoice and have some faith,
That Jesus left us to run this race;
With all power hand in hand.

RELIEF

There is relief when you know Jesus Christ,
Life's journey can knock you down;
It's real comfort when he's around,
There is relief when you know Jesus Christ;
To trust his judgment and know the best,
We have faith to finish the rest;
There is relief when you know he's there,
He helps you fight your daily battles;
No matter how far he must travel,
There is relief when you know he's there;
"Forgive them father,"
"For they know not what they do;"
You have given relief to those who love you too.

SAYING GOOD-BYE

Death is something we all have to face,
Along with Satan we are running a race;
It may take one of our love ones away,
And that makes us want to cry;
Especially when we are saying good-bye
It will hurt us, we know that for sure,
Knowing God's word will make us pure;
So all we have to do is keep the faith,
As we continue in God's Holy grace;
Because one of these day's we will see them again,
And we can ask them how have they been;
In a wonderful, marvelous, spiritual place.

THE LIGHT

The light will show you,
The things you have never seen before;
You may hear somethings you,
Have never heard before;
You may meet some people,
You have never met before;
The light will comfort you,
When you have done no wrong;
And when trouble comes on ever hand,
The light is there to guide you;
Through the heart aches of the world,
The disappointments at every turn;
The misunderstood on everything,
The light will show you;
That there is a way,
But you must fast and pray;
Let Jesus be the light for you,
He can guide you through the night;
And when morning comes around again,
You can trust and believe, keep the faith;
That Jesus Christ is The Light.

TRUST

Trust in him who will not leave you,
Trust in him who will always care,
Trust in him who will believe you,
Trust in him who will be there;
Trust you need from the beginning,
Trust you need to have the faith,
Trust you need to keep on winning,
Trust you need to finish the race;
Trust in him that loves you so,
Trust in him that cares so much,
Trust in him that will let you know,
To trust in him and never let go.

UNITY

Unity starts with Jesus Christ,
Once you know him, you will want to do right;
Unity is staying on one accord,
To please the one and only Lord;
Unity is always agreeing on things,
No matter how much trouble it brings;
Unity is love, wrapped up tight,
It has no room for fuss or fight;
Unity is saying I care for you,
Always showing and expressing it too;
Unity began with Jesus Christ,
Because he showed us his marvelous light.

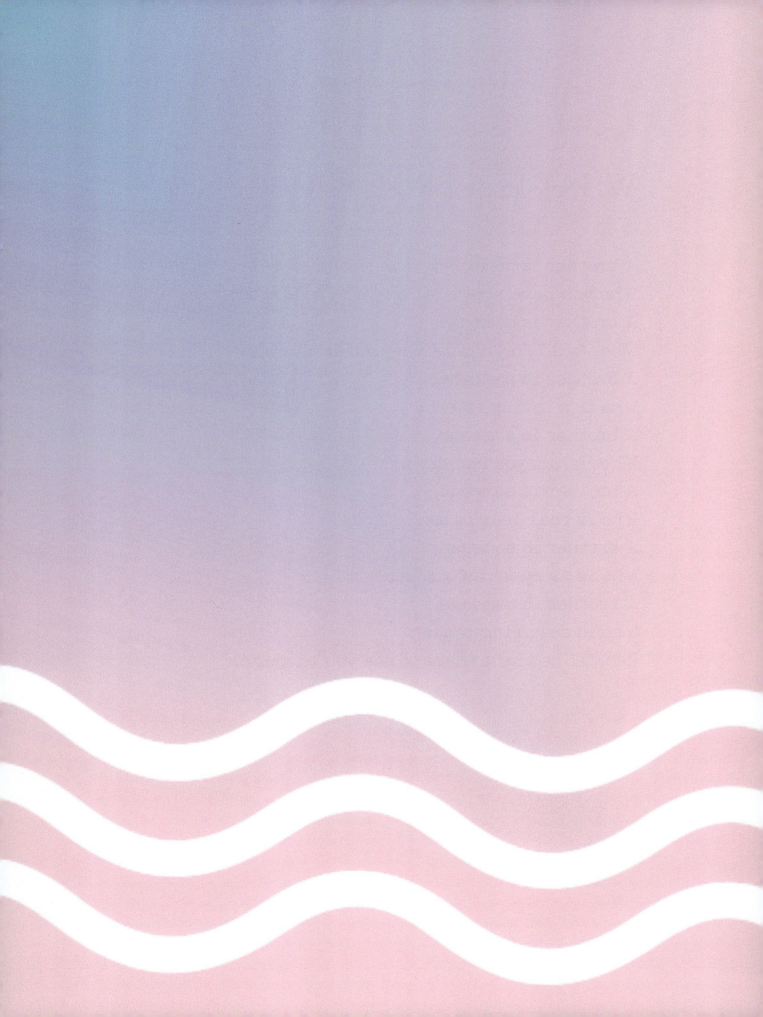

WHAT IS A BROTHER

A brother is someone,
Who you have known since your childhood;
A brother is someone,
Who would do whatever he could;
A brother is someone,
Who is a loving friend;
A brother is someone,
Who in him you can depend;
A brother is someone,
Who is real dear to me;
A brother is someone,
Who is as sweet as can be;
A brother is someone,
Who is so caring to you;
He will be right there to see you through.

WHAT IS A HUSBAND

A husband is someone,
Who you know as a friend;
A husband is someone,
Who you have married to the end;
A husband is someone,
Who you love, oh so dear;
A husband is someone,
Who has found a love real near;
A husband is someone,
Who God has given from above;
A husband is someone,
Who you really truly love;
A husband is someone,
Who is there through thick and thin;
You both have vowed to the end,
A life together;
In sickness and in health,
Forsaken all others and to love;
One another.

WHAT IS GOD TRYING TO SAY?

WHAT IS GOD TRYING TO SAY,
WHEN YOU WORK SO HARD,
LIVE LIFE DAY BY DAY,
AND LOVE THOSE THAT COME YOUR WAY;
WHAT IS GOD TRYING TO SAY,
WHEN THOSE YOU LOVE,
FOR SOME STRANGE REASON, THEY GET ILL,
AND YOU LOOK TOWARDS HEAVEN TO SEE HIS WILL;
WHAT IS GOD TRYING TO SAY,
WHEN YOU ARE FACED ALL ALONE,
AND YOU FEEL LIKE SOMETHING,
HAS GONE TERRIBLY WRONG;
WHAT IS GOD TRYING TO SAY,
YOU COME OUT SMILING,
FROM CHEEK TO CHEEK,
AND STILL ON FIRE FOR THE LORD,
AND WONDERING AT THE SAME TIME,
WHAT IS GOD TRYING TO SAY.

WIPE THE TEARS

Wipe the tears from your eyes,
So you can see that God is alive;
Wipe the tears from your eyes,
Because now you know that by and by;
Wipe the tears from your eyes,
That God is always by your side;
Wipe the tears from your eyes,
You know that God will be your guide;
Wipe the tears from your eyes,
Because now you know you can survive;
Wipe the tears from your eyes,
So you can see that God is alive.

WISDOM

Wisdom is something that makes you strong,
It teaches you right from wrong;
Wisdom is something that comes day by day,
It helps you along the way;
Wisdom is something that makes you aware,
It shows you the things to beware;
Wisdom is something that gives you faith,
It will guide you to God's good grace;
Wisdom is something we all must have,
It will help us along our paths;
Wisdom will lead us to a marvelous life,
And we can get to know;
Our Lord and Savior Jesus Crist.

YOU CAN MAKE IT

YOU CAN MAKE IT,
JUST TAKE ONE DAY AT A TIME,
WHICH IS THE KEY;
YOU CAN MAKE IT,
THROUGH LIFE'S CHALLENGES;
YOU CAN MAKE IT,
UP THOSE TALL, ROUGH MOUNTAINS;
YOU CAN MAKE IT,
ACROSS THE WIDE RIVERS TOO,
FROM OCEAN TO OCEAN;
YOU CAN MAKE IT,
LOOKING ONE DAY FROM EAST TO WEST,
AND PICTURING THE ROUTE FROM NORTH TO SOUTH;
YOU CAN MAKE IT,
OH LIFE ISN'T EASY,
OUR JOURNEY'S WE MUST PLAN,
FOR THEY SHOULD GO HAND IN HAND,
WITH THE GOD I KNOW,
WHO REIGNS UP ABOVE,
WHO WILL STAY WITH YOU AND ME,
HE WILL SHOW HIS LOVE,
AND THEN YOU WILL KNOW FOR SURE,
THAT YOU CAN MAKE IT.

YOUR LIFE IS IN THE DARK

You have went through something different in your life,
So now your life is in the dark;
All your hope is gone from you,
So now your life is in the dark;
Your friends have turned and walked away,
So now your life is in the dark;
Your family you had, have all gone mad,
So now your life is in the dark;
The security you had it's gone bad,
So now your life is in the dark;
The life you knew, just hang on to,
Because Jesus knew you would someday feel that way;
But just remember God is the way,
The truth and the light;
Don't be alarm if your life is in the dark,
It will soon be light again.